Copyright © 2005 by Mary F. Pecci

All rights reserved.
No part of this book may be reproduced
without written consent of the author.

First Edition
ISBN 978-0-943220-13-0

Distributed by:
PECCI EDUCATIONAL PUBLISHERS
www.onlinereadingteacher.com
sales@onlinereadingteacher.com

Other Books by Mary F. Pecci
At Last! A Reading Method for EVERY Child! - NEW SIMPLIFIED EDITION
At Last! A Reading Method for EVERY Child! - READING SPECIALIST EDITION
Why Johnny Ain't Never Gonna Read (A Challenge to the Nation)
How to Discipline Your Class for Joyful Teaching
5 Steps to Save Our Schools

Pecci Reading Series
Pre-Primer I
Pre-Primer II
Pre-Primer III
Primer
1^1 Reader

Super Spelling
Book One

Super Seatwork
Letter-Recognition
Color Words
Number Words
Content Areas
Phonic Grab Bag
Linguistic Exercises
Word Skills

This Pre-Primer is designed to be used in conjunction with:
At Last! A Reading Method for EVERY Child!

ACKNOWLEDGMENTS

This reading series is dedicated to my beloved brother, Dr. Ernest F. Pecci, and his remarkable daughter, Diana Pecci La Brecque, who set this project into motion by saying those magic words, "Yes! You CAN do it!"

Sincere appreciation also goes to my sister, Marguerite Pecci Kelley, for her story suggestions and for always being on call to backboard ideas.

And a very special thanks goes to June Triesch, quintessential Kindergarten teacher, who retired on her 80th birthday, about whom such teachers it has been written, "God doesn't have hands; He uses the teacher's hands," for her constant faithfulness over the years as dearest friend and mentor.

Teacher's Guide

Pages 49 - 52

Vocabulary Word List - p. 49

Word-for-Word Dialogue
between Teacher and Student - p. 50 - 52

In this reader, 25 words are formally introduced. However, reading vocabulary will not be limited to these 25 words because students will be acquiring independent decoding skills as they progress through this reader. This reader serves only as a springboard, from which students will be able to read *any* material on (and in most cases above) their academic level.

John

Kim

Sam

Pam

Hi, I am John.

Hi, I am Kim.

Hi, I am Sam.

Hi, I am Pam.

Hi!

Hi, I am Pam.
Hi, I am Kim.

Hi, I am John.
Hi, I am Sam.

Hi, I am Kim.
Hi, I am Sam.

Hi, I am Pam.
Hi, I am John.

Look at Kim.

Look at Pam.

Look at John.

Look at Sam.

Look

Look, Kim.

Oh, oh, oh!

Oh, look, John

Look at that!

The

Look, Pam.

Look at that.

Look at the  .

Look, Pam.

Now look at the .

Look at that.

Look, Sam.

Now look at the ⊕.

Look at that.

Oh, oh, Pam.

Oh, Sam.

Look at the ⊗ now.

Look at that!

Bo Bo

Come, Bo Bo.
Look at the 🥣.
Look at the 🔫.
Come, Bo Bo, come.
Come, come.

Oh, oh!
Look at Bo Bo.
Look at the ⌐━━▷ now.
Look at John and Bo Bo.
Look at the ⌐━━▷ .

Look at the 🚿 now.
Look at John now.
Look at Bo Bo now.

Oh, oh!
Look at John and Bo Bo now.
Come, Bo Bo, come.

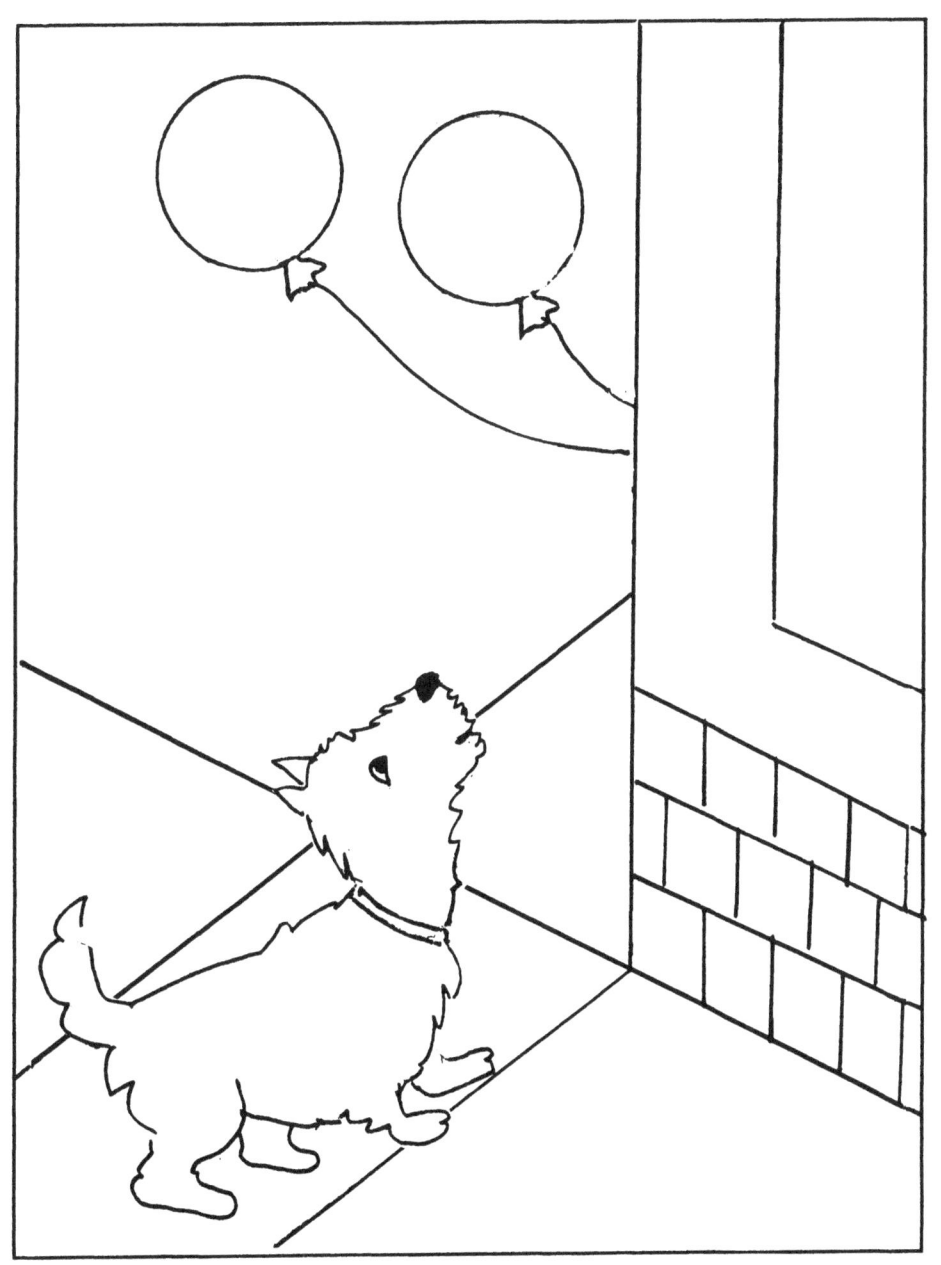

Bo Bo and the

Hi, Bo Bo.
Come, come.
Look up, up, up.
Look up at the  .
Look at Kim and Pam
Come, Bo Bo, come.

Down, Bo Bo.
Down, down, down.
Look up at the 🎈.
Look at Pam and Kim.
Down, Bo Bo, down.
Down, down, down.

Now look at Bo Bo.
Now look at the 🎈.
Look up, up, up.
Look at Bo Bo and the 🎈 now.
Come, Bo Bo.
Come, Bo Bo, come.

Scratch

Come, Scratch, come.

Look up, up, up.

Look at Sam and the 🫧.

Come, come, Scratch.

Look at the 🫧 go up.

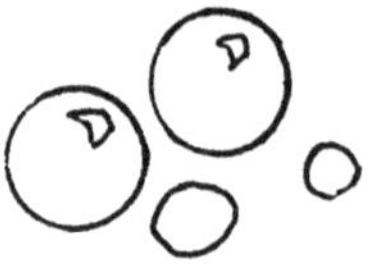

Up, up, up.

Go, go, go.

Look down, Scratch.
Now the ◯ ◯ go down.
Down, down, down.

Come, Scratch, come.
Jump up at the ◯ ◯ .
Jump, jump, jump.
Go, go, go.

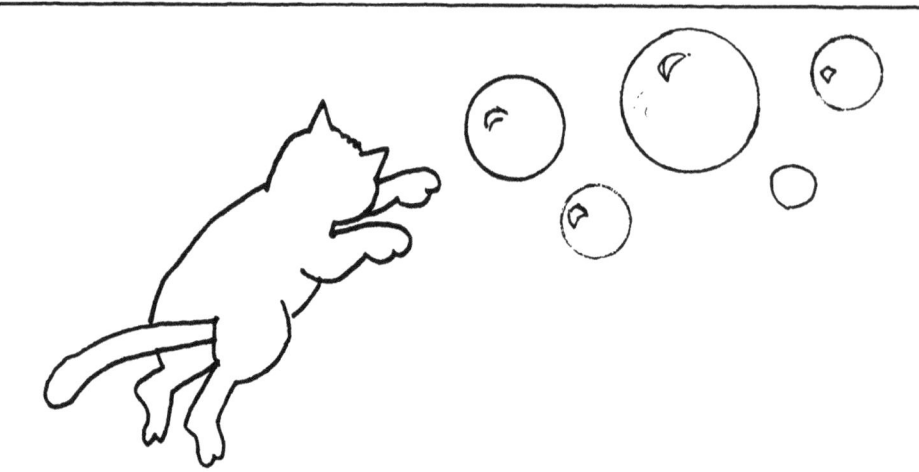

Scratch can jump.
Scratch can jump up.
Scratch can jump up at the ⬭.

Oh, oh, oh!
Look at Scratch now.
Look at Scratch and the ⬭.

Scratch and the

Look at Scratch jump.
Scratch can jump up.
Scratch can jump down.
Up and down.
Up and down.
Look at Scratch go.
Up and down.

Oh, oh.

Look at Scratch now.

Look at Scratch and the .

Look at that.

Look at Sam.

Come, Scratch, come.

Come now, Scratch.

Come, Scratch, come.

Look at Sam now.

Look at that.

Look at Sam and the  .

Now look at Scratch go!

Go,

    go,

        go!

Play

Hi, John. Look at the 🏐.
The 🏐 can go up and down.
Come and play 🏐.

Hi Sam.
I can play 🏐.

Look at the 🏀 now.
Look at the 🏀 go up.
Go, 🏀, go!

Jump up, John.
Look at the 🏀 go up.
Jump up, up, up.
Go, John, go!

Oh, oh, John.
Look at that dog.
The dog can jump up, up, up.
The dog can play 🎾.

Oh, Sam!
Bo Bo can play 🎾.
Look at that dog.

Kim and Pam Play

Look at Pam and Kim.
Look at the big  .
Now Kim and Pam can play  .

Look at the 🎩. 
Look at the 👠👠. 
Look at Kim and Pam.
Kim is big now.
Pam is big now.
Kim and Pam can play .

Hi, Bo Bo. Hi, Scratch.

Come Bo Bo.
Come and play 🏠.

Come Scratch.
Come and play 🏠.

Now look at big Bo Bo.
Now look at big Scratch.

Look at Bo Bo jump.
Up, up, up.

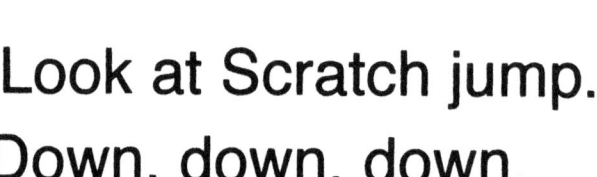

Look at Scratch jump.
Down, down, down.

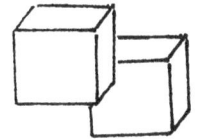

The Big 🧊

Sam and John can play 🧊.

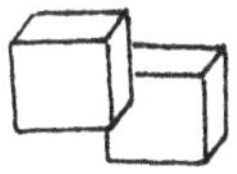

Look at the 🧊 go up.

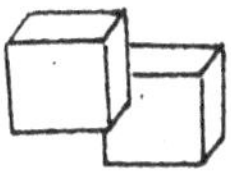

The big 🧊 go up, up, up.

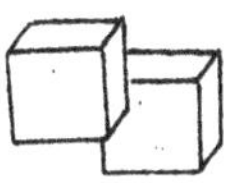

Look at Sam and John play 🧊.

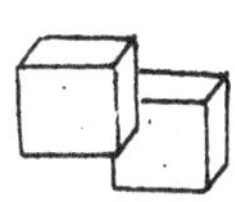

Come, Bo Bo, come.

Look at the 🦮 .

Come now, Bo Bo.

Come now.

Come, come, come, Bo Bo.

Look at the 🦮 .

John and Sam can play 🧊.
Look at the big 🔺.
Look at that!
The 🔺 is big, big, big.
The 🔺 is up, up, up.
Now look at the big, big 🔺.

Oh, oh! Look at that dog.
Now the big 🧊 is down.
Down, down, down.
Look at the big 🧊 come down!
Go, Bo Bo, go!

Pre-Primer I
Vocabulary Word List

Page 4 - John
          Kim
          Sam
          Pam

Pages 5 - 8

p. 5 - Hi
       I *
       am

Pages 9 - 12

p. 12 - Look
        at

Pages 13 - 16

p. 15 - Oh
p. 16 - that

Pages 17 - 20

p. 17 - The
p. 18 - now (**ow**) **

Pages 21 - 24

p, 21 - Bo Bo
p. 22 - Come
p. 23 - and

Pages 25 - 28

p. 26 - up
p. 27 - down

Pages 29 - 32

p. 29 - Scratch
p. 30 - go
p. 31 - Jump
p. 32 - can

Pages 33 - 36

(Absorption Story)

Pages 37 - 40

p. 37 - play (**ay**) ***
p. 39 - dog

Pages 41 - 44

p. 41 - big
p. 42 - is

Pages 45 - 48

(Absorption Story)

  * A Word Card is not needed for this word.
 ** Introduce the "**ow**" Sight Family beforehand.
*** Introduce the "**ay**" Sight Family beforehand.

Word-for-Word Dialogue

Before beginning this reader, complete the <u>Pre-Requisite Skills</u> in *At Last! A Reading method for EVERY Child*, p. 29-94. Be sure to review the Pre-Requisite Flashcard review every day, p. 94. (Post it for easy reference.)

Before introducing the new words for each story in this reader, read p. 99-118 in *At Last!*. Be sure to follow the directions, which are summarized below:

---

1. Write a list of the words to be introduced that day for the assigned pages, as illustrated on p. 99-101 in *At Last!*.

2. Introduce the words as scripted below.

3. Review the Word List as per the NOTE on top of p. 112 of *At Last!*.

4. Put the words introduced on flashcards and review them each day *before* introducing new words. (No word cards are needed after the Pre-Primers.)

5. Reinforce words with the Word Reinforcement activities on p. 135-140 in *At Last!* and apply the Pre-Requisite skills reinforcement activities to words.

Now, you are ready to begin!

Following is the word-for-word dialogue between teacher and student for introducing every word in this reader:

<u>Page 4</u>

	Teacher:	**Student:**
John -	This boy's name is "John." What's the clue?	<u>J</u> <u>o</u> h <u>n</u>
Kim -	This girl's name is "Kim." What's the clue?	<u>K</u> i <u>m</u>
Sam -	This boy's name is "Sam." What's the clue?	<u>S</u> a <u>m</u>
Pam -	This girl's name is "Pam." What's the clue?	<u>P</u> a <u>m</u>

<u>Pages 5 - 8</u>

Hi -	Another way to say "hello" is - What's the clue?	H i <u>H</u> i
I -	This word is "I," as in "<u>I</u> am John." What's the clue?	 <u>I</u>
am -	Do you know who I - What's the clue?	a m <u>a</u> <u>m</u>

<u>Pages 9 - 12</u>

	Teacher:	**Student:**
Look -	Open your eyes and take a good - What's the clue?	L o o k <u>L</u> o o <u>k</u>
at -	What are you looking - What's the clue?	a t <u>a</u> <u>t</u>

<u>Pages 13 - 16</u>

Oh -	This word is "Oh," as in "<u>Oh</u>, look at that!" What's the clue?	<u>O</u> h
that -	Don't look at this - look at - What's the clue?	t h a t <u>t h</u> <u>a t</u>

<u>Pages 17 - 20</u>

The -	This word is "the," as in "Look at <u>the</u> ball." What's the clue?	<u>T h</u> e

NOTE: Introduce the Sight Family "**ow**" <u>during the</u> <u>Phonic</u> <u>Period</u> before introducing the next word.

now -	Underline O-W. What's the Sight Family? What's the word?	<u>o w</u> o w n o w

<u>Pages 21 - 24</u>

Bo Bo -	The dog's name is "Bo Bo." What's the clue?	<u>B</u> o <u>B</u> o
Come -	When I call you, I want you to - What's the clue?	c o m e <u>c</u> o <u>m</u> e
and -	This word is "and," as in "Look at John <u>and</u> Bo Bo." What's the clue?	<u>a</u> <u>n</u> <u>d</u>

<u>Pages 25 - 28</u>

up -	The ball went down and the ball went - What's the clue?	u p <u>u</u> <u>p</u>
down -	The ball went up and the ball went - What's the clue?	d o w n <u>d</u> <u>o w</u> <u>n</u>

<u>Pages 29 - 32</u>

Scratch -	The cat's name is "Scratch." What's the clue?	<u>S</u> <u>c</u> r a t <u>ch</u>
go -	Get ready because it's time to - What's the clue?	g o <u>g</u> <u>o</u>
Jump -	A rabbit can hop and - What's the clue?	J u m p <u>J</u> <u>u</u> <u>m</u> p
can -	Can you do this? Yes, you - What's the clue?	c a n <u>c</u> <u>a</u> <u>n</u>

Pages 33 - 36

(Absorption Story)

Pages 37 - 40

Teacher: **Student:**

NOTE: Introduce the "**ay**" Sight Family <u>during the Phonic Period</u> before introducing the next word.

play -	Underline A-Y.	<u>a y</u>
	What's the Sight Family?	a y
	What's the word?	p l a y
dog -	My pet is a -	d o g
	What's the clue?	d <u>o</u> g

Pages 41 - 44

big -	If it's not little, it must be -	b i g
	What's the clue?	b <u>i</u> g
is -	Do you know what this -	i s
	What's the clue?	i <u>s</u>

(**Note:** Exaggerate the sound of "s" to assist decoding.)

Pages 45 - 48

(Absorption Story)

* * * * * * * * * * * * * * * * * *